The Oxford Piano Method

SPOOKY PIANO TIME

Terrifying Pieces, Poems, and Puzzles

by

Pauline Hall and Kevin Wooding

Illustrated by Chris Mould

T0057024

Music Department
OXFORD UNIVERSITY PRESS
Oxford and New York

Oxford University Press, Great Clarendon Street, Oxford OX2 6DP, England

Oxford New York
Auckland Bangkok Buenos Aires Cape Town Chennai
Dar es Salaam Delhi Hong Kong Istanbul Karachi Kolkata
Kuala Lumpur Madrid Melbourne Mexico City Mumbai
Nairobi São Paulo Shanghai Taipei Tokyo Toronto

Oxford is a trade mark of Oxford University Press

25

ISBN 978-0-19-372765-6

Music and text originated by Barnes Music Engraving Limited, East Sussex, England

Printed by Halstan & Co. Ltd., Amersham, Bucks, England

Illustrations by Chris Mould

Poems by Kevin Wooding

Contents

The House on the Hill

The staccato notes need to be really short—some of them have accents too. If you can count lines and spaces, it's easy to work out what the last six notes should be!

KEVIN WOODING

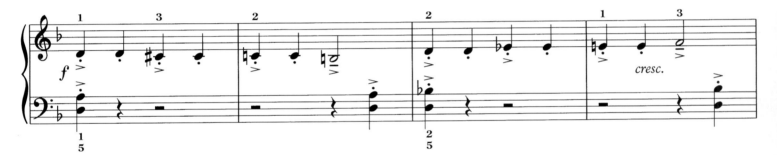

Work out all these leger lines before you play! →

Hush! while I tell of the House on the Hill
a dark and unwholesome and scary abode.
Nobody lives there—nobody will,
but vampires and werewolves, black bats and a toad.

The House on the Hill, the House on the Hill,
it's terrific, horrific: survival is nil.
The shrieks of the banshees, the wailing of ghouls
strike terror in all but the bravest of fools!

5

Meet the Family

This family are certainly a spooky and eccentric bunch of people! The piece needs to be light and swing along—but don't try to play it too fast.

KEVIN WOODING

When the sun is going down
and the light is growing dim,
the family creep up from the vaults,
Pasty-faced and grisly grim.

If you're brave enough you'll see
all the ghouls you just awoke,
a vampire and a pair of trolls
and many other gruesome folk.

So come on, meet the family!
(But please excuse me if I run,
for I know that once they've started
all these eerie 'dear departed'
won't stop until they've scared the
daylights out of everyone!)

Compose a Creepy Piece

It's really easy. First put your right hand over these notes:

and your left hand on these two: (play them an octave lower for a spooky sound.)

Now hold down the left-hand chord while your right hand plays a creepy tune using the five notes played in any order. Play them very quietly (*pp*). Keep the sustain pedal down all the time—it gives a great effect!

Try repeating the left-hand chord and turn your piece into a sort of ghoulish march. Try some different ways of playing your piece but remember IT MUST SOUND SCARY!

Vampire Blues

You must count steadily and carefully—rests are very important, and there are lots of them. Beware of the vampire's 'bite' near the end!

KEVIN WOODING

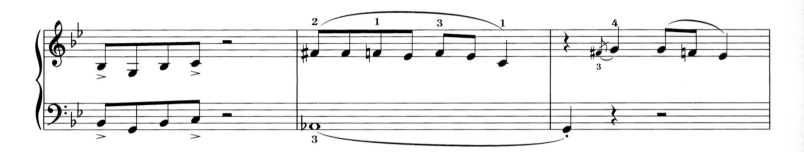

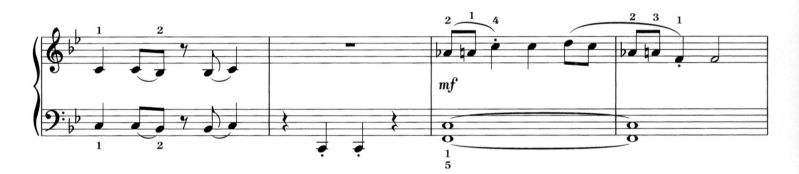

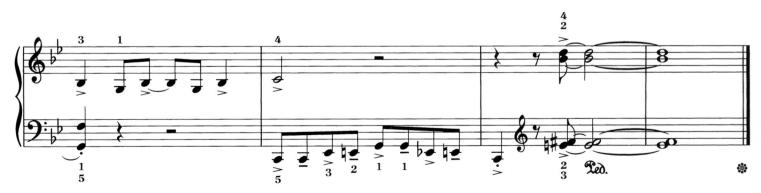

Grampa Vampire, tall and lank,
prowling round in places dank,

Loves to rest his head in mould,
dirt and cobwebs round him fold,

Partial to a chew of mud,
but only when he can't get blood!

By day he sleeps down in the crypt,
with pleasant dreams of those he's nipped,

Inside a coffin, hid from sight,
his body cold and chalky-white.

Now midnight strikes and up he rises
sporting fearsome sharp incisors.

He has a victim in his sights,
creeps up slowly, smiles, then
BITES!

Lydia's Sandwich

Don't be put off by all those flats—they're really easy once you know where to position your hands. For most of the piece your left hand only plays three different notes. Watch out for the really high notes at the end. The left hand sounds really good if played an octave lower throughout.

KEVIN WOODING

Creepy and Crawly

Leave out the F if you ↓ can't stretch to it!

This means play two octaves higher than written. → *15ma*

Take twenty-seven wriggly worms
a cup of purple slime
mix them in a chamber pot
then add a twist of lime.

Grab a jar of spiders and a
slice of mouldy bread,
spread the filling and the bugs
on top, then SQUASH 'EM DEAD!

YUM!

Sandwich Puzzle

Lydia's ghoul-friends have popped round for tea. They're having sandwiches but someone has muddled up all the letters on the sandwich labels. Can you rearrange the letters to spell the name of each sandwich?

Each glass has a **key signature** drawn on it. Can you name which **major** key it is? Write the answer in the space at the top of the glass.

SEECHE AND MISLE

BRAC MAJ

YADIL`S WINDSACH

DUM AND NEHOY

GLUS TUTREB

MAH AND CHATCOOLE

John Brown's Funeral March

Although 2/2 means two minim beats in a bar, you should count out four crotchets to begin with. Make the low left-hand chord sound like a deep bell tolling.

Grave (Alla marcia)

PAULINE HALL

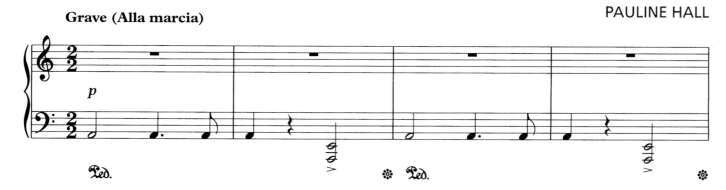

A funeral is often a gloomy affair
but none are so gruesome as this one,
the House on the Hill has more than its share—
a day won't go by that they miss one.

The pall-bearers march up the gravel each morn
even if no one has died;
'what does that matter?' they say to themselves,
'we'll put someone living inside!'

The screams which come out are annoying of course
so the lid is nailed shut good and tight,
and as the procession moves off to the church
it's truly a spine-chilling sight.

'So bring out your dead! Bring out your dead!
And bring out some living ones too!
As soon as we get to the end of this list
we'll be starting another with you!'

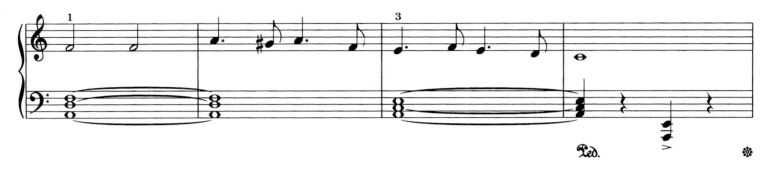

Rupert

You should play this quite heavily and with plenty of accents. Try the left-hand part an octave lower throughout to sound like mad-bad-Rupert revving his bike!

KEVIN WOODING

Rupert, Rupert, super-cool,
never has to go to school.

Always does just as he likes,
and rides on ghostly motorbikes.

With deafening roar and clouds of smoke
he puts the wind up mortal folk.

Back from Heaven (or maybe Hades . . .?)
to scare the boys and WOW! the ladies.

Super Rupert, you're the most
scary, hairy, quite contrary,
death-defying (watch him flying!)
G . . . G . . . G . . . G . . . G . . . G . . . GHOST!

The Egyptian Level

To keep all those hungry mummies happy you must make this piece as smooth and snaky as you possibly can!

KEVIN WOODING

Mummies here,
mummies there,
mummies in their underwear.

Drinking coffee,
eating pie,
lying in sarcophagi.

No, not mothers
(as you thought),
but mummies of the other sort.

Bandaged beasties
from Khartoum,
yes, Egyptians in this room.

Although they may be
eating pie,
I think that you had better fly . . .

For ravenous relics
love to munch
and might mistake you for their lunch!

Lady Eleanor

The tune in the right hand must really sing out, so keep the left-hand accompaniment as quiet as you can. Play the right hand an octave higher throughout.

KEVIN WOODING

Cantabile

Come into the valley
where you hear the distant bell,
cast your gaze across the flowers
covering the dell.

You find your eyes are misty,
your thoughts are hard to keep,
you try to stay awake, but soon
you slowly drift to sleep . . .

And in your trance you see the flowers
floating through the air,
guided by a ghostly hand . . .
Lady Eleanor is there.

A noble woman, lost in time
her face appears to yearn,
she waits and waits but cannot rest
until her lord's return.

Frightening Phrases

Each of these frightening phrases has its own rhythm and each of these rhythms are written out for you somewhere on the page. Can you match up the rhythms with their frightening phrases? Write each correct number in the right box and carry on!

Phantango

A tango is a type of dance, so the rhythm here must be very steady. Look out for *pp subito* in the music—ask your teacher what it means. Play the left-hand part an octave lower except for the last two bars.

PETER GRITTON

↑ *Ped.*
This means play at
the written pitch again.

Come dance the Phantango with me
in the moonlight, around the marquee,
we'll feast upon mangos,
and 'bing' on some bongos,
from eight until quarter to three.

Some witches appear with Phantabulous hair
who dance with both daring and flair,
just watch them mix rumba
with salsa and samba
while floating about in mid-air!

So dance the Phantango tonight,
you needn't feel all of a fright,
if some spook should shout 'Boo!'
Just reply: 'Same to you!
You phantoms should be more polite!'

21

Sweet Dreams

Don't be frightened!—after the scary first bar (which returns to haunt you in the fourth line),
this piece becomes a quiet and dreamy lullaby. Make it sleepy and smooth and try not to rush.

KEVIN WOODING

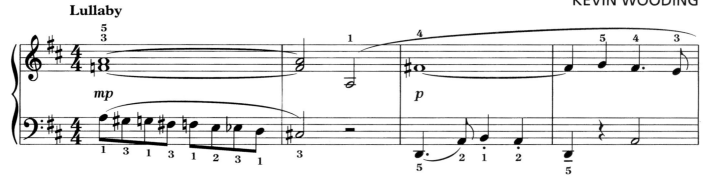

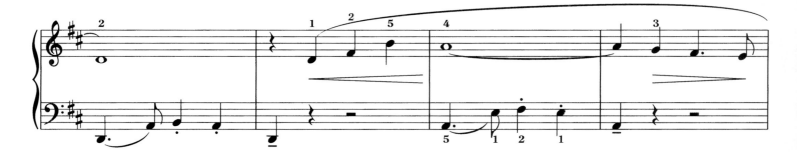

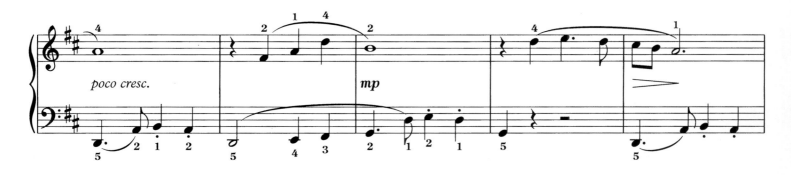

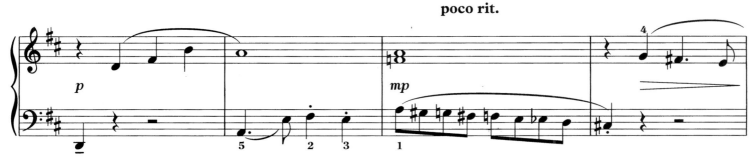

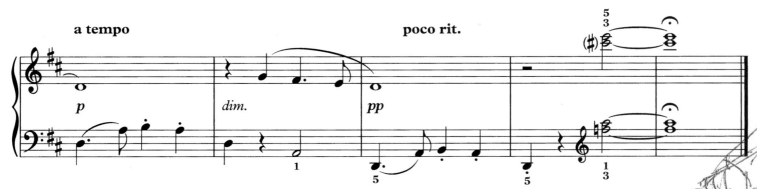

Now night has come, it's time for bed
where you can rest your sleepy head.
No need to think of horrid beasts,
But dream instead of . . .
. . . midnight feasts

Or far-off lands . . .
. . . with willow trees
some sunny fields . . .
. . . and deep-blue seas

The lights are out, the door ajar,
familiar sounds come from afar.

Voices slowly change to streams
flowing out into your dreams,
and dreams turn into rivers deep,
for now you're safe, and sound asleep . . .

Escape from the House on the Hill

To escape from the haunted House on the Hill to safety you must follow one of the treacherous winding paths below. But BEWARE: if your path is blocked by a vampire bat you must complete the task on the scroll before moving on. Try out all the routes—if you dare!